# Making Music with a Hearing Loss
## Strategies and Stories

*Edited by Cherisse W. Miller, DMA*

AAMHL Publications
Rockville, Maryland

Library of Congress Cataloging-in-Publication Data
Miller, Cherisse W.
    Making Music with a Hearing Loss: Strategies and Stories
    ISBN 978-1-45658-638-6
    1. Music   2. Hearing Loss   I. Miller, Cherisse W.   II. Title.

# Contributors

Brad Ingrao, AuD.
*e-audiology.net*

Marshall Chasin, AuD., M.Sc., Aud(C), Reg. CASLPO
*Musicians Clinics of Canada*
*Toronto, Canada*

Jennifer Castellano
*Thornwood, New York*

Wendy Cheng
*Gaithersburg, Maryland*

Joan Ernst
*Hertford, North Carolina*

Mike McConnell
*Battle Ground, Washington*

Erin McKenzie-Christiansen
*Adelaide, Australia*

Cherisse Miller, DMA
*Columbia, South Carolina*

Renee O'Connell
*Charlottesville, Virginia*

Tim Polashek, PhD
*Lexington, Kentucky*

Janice Rosen
*Washington, D.C.*

Lisa Smith
*St. Louis, Missouri*

Ali Zimmerman
*Indianapolis, Indiana*

# Contents

# Foreward

Growing up in North Carolina in the 1970s with a significant hearing loss, I knew I was different from my peers in public school. Not only did I not hear well, I was also an athletic klutz who was always the last person to be picked on a sport team. While I heard and read about hearing-impaired peers making names for themselves by excelling in sports and visual arts, I was intrigued with music. My mother arranged for me to take classical piano lessons as a child and I started violin lessons in college. I even passed a musical aptitude exam enabling me to participate in the seventh grade band.

However, I had no real role models to look up to or network with. There were no fellow hearing-impaired musicians to commiserate with me on the problems of following a teacher's instructions in recorder class as she walked around the room with her back turned, or coping with a high school choral director's curt assessment that I was absolutely incapable of singing in tune because of my hearing loss. In 2001 I sat in a workshop at a Self Help for Hard of Hearing (SHHH) convention where a music therapist did a presentation on her techniques for teaching hearing-impaired children how to appreciate music. Keep in mind that that she was speaking to an audience of hearing-impaired adults—several of whom were skilled musicians in their own right.

After my children were born I wanted to be able to hear their voices, and began looking into getting a cochlear implant. Cochlear implant audiologists told me that the first priority for programming speech processors were for speech perception, and that music perception with cochlear implants was not seen as a priority in the hearing health care field. No one seemed to take seriously the problems and needs of hearing-impaired adults who not only appreciated music, but also desired to integrate music in their lives by playing or performing music.

The above experiences were major factors in my decision to form the Association of Adult Musicians with Hearing Loss (http://www.aamhl.org) in 2001. Here, via the power of the Internet, we can exchange information on making music with a hearing loss, discuss strategies on integrating hearing loss into our musical lives, and network with other musicians with hearing loss. Audiologists and music educators interested in working with hearing-impaired music students also join in this information exchange. Here at last, we find kindred souls who share our mutual passion for making and performing music and face similar barriers in keeping music in our lives as hearing-impaired individuals.

Wendy Cheng
*Founder and President*
*Association of Adult Musicians with Hearing Loss*
*Rockville, Maryland*
March 2011

# Preface

This book is our Association's first venture into publishing and demonstrating our combined expertise on hearing loss and experiences on making music with a hearing loss. Chapter 1 discusses how we hear sound. Chapter 2 discusses the capabilities and limitations of using today's hearing devices in playing music. Chapter 3 is a brief overview of hearing conservation for musicians. Chapter 4 is a compilation of real life experiences by eleven adult hard of hearing or deaf musicians who share their personal stories and strategies of how they continue to integrate music-making in their lives.

Putting together this inaugural edition required a lot of collaboration. The Association gratefully thanks Dr. Brad Ingrao for writing chapter 1 and to Dr. Marshall Chasin for writing chapters 2 and 3. We thank the many musicians with hearing loss who eagerly sent in their stories for chapter 4.

It is our hope that through our stories, adults with hearing loss will be inspired to experience for themselves the joy of making music.

Cherisse Miller, DMA
*Columbia, South Carolina*
March 2011

CHAPTER 1

# Hearing

*Brad Ingrao, AuD.*

The human auditory system is a complex system of harmonics, mechanics and neuro-electronics. Each component has a specific purpose, but like an orchestra, these work together to create more than the sum of the parts.

This chapter describes the auditory system from the "outside–in," including the function and contribution in the experience of hearing and understanding.

## Anatomy

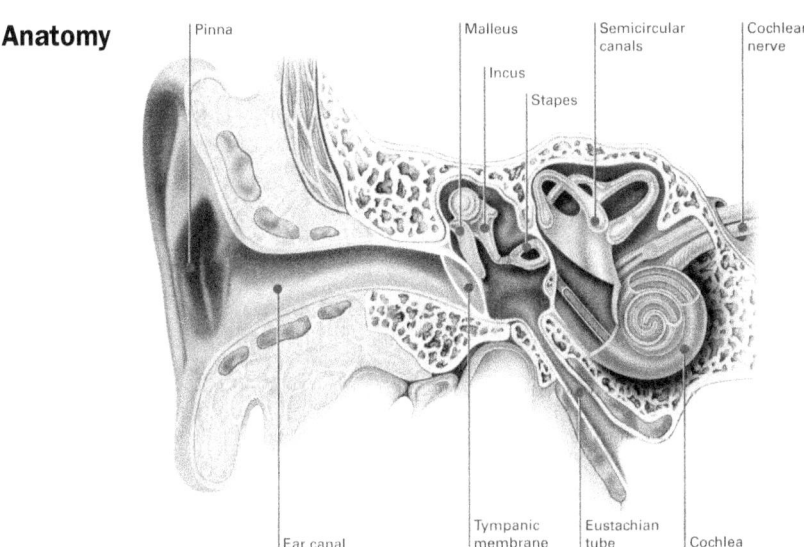

Figure 1-1: A cut away view of the outer, middle and inner ear. See text for more information. Figure courtesy of Bernafon-Canada. Used with permission.

The ear is divided into two major segments, the peripheral and central. The peripheral auditory system is further divided into the outer, middle and inner ear. Let's look at each part.

## The Outer Ear

The outer ear includes the pinna and the external ear canal. These structures function primarily as funnels and resonators, but also protect the delicate structures of the middle and inner ear from foreign objects.

The primary purpose of the pinna is to collect sounds in the air. Collecting sound energy over a large area and delivering that energy to a smaller area (the ear canal) increases the sound pressure of the sound. This increased sound pressure is perceived as an increase in loudness.

Take a look at your pinna. See all those ridges and grooves? Each of these diffracts (bends) sound differently depending on the frequency. This diffraction helps the brain make estimates of location, amplitude and phasing for the purpose of localizing sounds.

After being collected by the pinna, sounds travel down the external ear canal. The ear canal is a closed tube about 2.5 cm long in adults and behaves acoustically like a single tube in a Pan flute (or empty soda bottle). The size and geometry of human ear canals results in significant resonant peaks at about 2700 Hz for adults and about 4000 Hz for children. Ear canal resonance is also important for hearing protection. The end of the ear canal marks the border between the outer ear and the middle ear.

## The Middle Ear

At the far inside end of the ear canal we find the tympanic membrane, or eardrum. The eardrum further amplifies the incoming sounds in two ways. First, it vibrates like the head of a tympani drum. You can argue the chicken and egg aspects of who named it first with your local anatomists and musicologists, and then let us know who won. The eardrum vibrates and moves three tiny bones, the Hammer, the Anvil and the Stirrup (Malleus, Incus and Stapes for your trivia buffs). This movement amplifies the sounds and passes them on to the inner ear. In addition, each of these bones acts as a resonating rod, with a different harmonic frequency. The eardrum also has a resonant frequency. The sum of all these resonances as well as the difference in area between the eardrum and the end of the stirrup adds about 31 dB to the incoming sound.

An important, but often forgotten part of the middle ear is the Eustachian Tube, which connects the middle ear to the back of the nose (nasopharynx). Under normal circumstances, the Eustachian Tube opens each time we swallow and re-equalizes the pressure in the middle ear relative to the outside world. This equal pressure is necessary for the eardrum to vibrate freely and for the middle ear amplification to occur.

Eustachian Tube Dysfunction (ETD) is common in young children and people with chronic sinusitis. It causes a temporary hearing loss that affects lower frequencies more than highs, and can result in a sense of being "plugged up" or having one's voice coming from deep inside a barrel. This is not necessarily an urgent issue. However long term, untreated ETD can progress to middle ear effusion, or fluid in the ear, and possibly a middle ear infection (otitis media).

For musicians, ETD can affect hearing overtones and harmonies, and can be painful for wind players due to the already high amount of intra-oral pressure needed to play. Clarinet and saxophone players will be further bothered by ETD since this "ear plugging" makes the sound of the instrument carried via bone conduction (teeth on mouthpiece) seem louder than the sound of their and other instruments coming into their ears.

Those with chronic ETD should consult an audiologist and physician to evaluate and treat the root cause rather than simply addressing the symptoms.

**The Inner Ear**

The base of the stapes, known as the foot plate, fits into a bony niche called the oval window. This opening into the inner ear is covered with a thin membrane and responds to the vibrations of the stapes. These then cause the fluid inside the cochlea, a snail shaped tube inside the temporal bone, to move. This movement takes the form of a traveling wave along the flexible basilar membrane.

This membrane separates the middle (scale media) and lower (scale tympani) tubes of the cochlea. All along the basilar membrane, rows of sensory hair cells make up the Organ of Corti. The structures of this organ transduce (convert) the vibrations of the basilar membrane into nerve impulses as follows:

Inside the Organ of Corti are thousands of sensory hair cells grouped in rows. At any given point of the organ, there are three rows of Outer Hair Cells (OHC) and one row of Inner Hair Cells (IHC). The OHCs act as pre-amplifiers, increasing the amplitude of the basilar membrane movements by contracting and expanding along their narrow tube-like bodies. This movement creates a sound, called the otoacoustic emission (OAE), which audiologists can measure and record. A second function of the OHC is to assist the brain in fine tuning pitch perception.

When a sound is heard, the brain records which OHCs and IHCs are stimulated and makes an initial guess as to the pitch of the sound. Then the brain "turns off" OHCs in areas just adjacent to the best guess "critical band." If the amount of nerve impulse stays the same, then the brain knows that the majority of the sound must have come from the best guess critical band. If, however, the amount of nerve impulse is reduced, then those adjacent areas must also contain significant energy and sound.

After a few of these "call and response" runs, the brain has a very accurate idea of the frequency of the sound, and then forms a perception of pitch.

If we lose OHCs because of age, disease or trauma (e.g. loud noise), the call and response system becomes confused because the brain never gets an updated attendance report when OHCs become damaged and disappear. Loss of a few OHCs is not a big problem, but the more you lose, the worse your pitch perception becomes. For the average person, this means they mishear a few speech sounds. For musicians, this can be a career killer. We'll talk more about how to prevent OHC loss in chapter 2.

The second half of accurate hearing is the Inner Hair Cell. Regardless of the health and accuracy of the OHC system, the IHCs act like microphones, transducing (converting) the basilar membrane wave into nerve impulses. If the IHCs are also damaged, then, like a microphone with a torn diaphragm, the signal getting to the sound board (brain) will be distorted. No amount of amplification will "clean up" this signal completely; however certain technologies, which will be discussed in later chapters, will certainly help.

## Central Auditory System

Once the IHCs do their thing, the nerve impulse version of the sound we heard travels up the auditory nerve to several "weigh stations" in the brainstem. Here the signal is analyzed for timing, amplitude, loudness and pitch. The right and left ear's version of the sound are compared to determine location, and information is sent to, and received from, the memory, attention and emotional areas of the brain. Finally, the auditory cortex connects all the dots and declares that we've just heard A 440 and off we go to do it all again for the next sound. This finely tuned team works full time, 24/7/365 from the day we are born until the day we die.

CHAPTER 2

# Music, Speech and Hearing Devices

*Marshall Chasin, AuD., M.Sc., Aud(C), Reg. CASLPO*

Music is everywhere—in the home, the car, the theatre, while jogging, and even when trying to study. Speech too is everywhere, and given a choice between hearing music and hearing speech, I suspect that everyone would choose speech. Communication trumps entertainment. Many brain researchers argue that music helped to develop language, and language in turn, helped develop music. Identical parts of the brain are used when listening to speech and listening to music, and in fact, music can be thought of as merely another form of communication.

Brain scientists have studied both speech and music and found them to be very complex. Neither is understood well. We do know that much of speech is located in the left side of the brain (at least for the majority of people) while music shares many of its function on both the right side and the left side of the brain. The part of the brain that joins the left and right sides (called the corpus callosum) is actually thicker in musicians than non-musicians, suggesting the possibility that the interplay between the two sides may be more active for musicians than for non-musicians. Music tends to be routed through more "emotion centers" in the brain (such as the amygdala and certain parts of the cerebellum. Loud music and certain types of music elicit an emotional response that is sometimes missing with speech. Thankfully, we do not have to choose between music and speech. Although the brain is rather complex and we do not fully understand how we process music and speech, we know many things about the differences and similarities between music and speech.

The loudness of speech is about 65 decibels (usually written as dB). A decibel is a unit of how intense or loud something is. A whisper or the rustling of leaves is 20-30 dB, and a loud cymbal crash in an orchestra can easily be over 110 dB. A noisy bus or streetcar can be 80 dB, and a plane taking off (if you are unfortunate enough to be on the runway) is about 130 dB. The higher the number (in dB), the greater the intensity, and the greater the potential damage to one's hearing. This is why hearing aids and cochlear implants provide sound that never exceeds an uncomfortably loud level. It is important to make speech and music loud enough to hear, but not too loud.

Having said this, many people like loud music. Part of the reason is that certain types of music (such as rock) need to be loud, whereas other types are intended for a less noisy venue. Another reason is that louder sounds (whether its noise or music) can cause the emotion centers of our brain (such as the amygdala) to become quite active. We have all heard a gradual welling up of a crescendo as the music comes to a climax, and depending on our personalities, may have a tear in our eye.

When music is turned down, our ear's natural ability to focus or tune itself is improved. Yet, if music (or any noise) is too loud, it can hurt and potentially damage one's hearing. Also, loud music sometimes does not sound as clear—for example, it can sound like a radio station that has been tuned slightly off the radio station. It may be loud, but will be fuzzy (see Figure 2-1).

Figure 2-1: This blurred radio is a metaphor for how speech or music would sound if the volume was too loud. Our hearing mechanism simply cannot handle overly loud sounds without some distortion. Used with permission, Musicians' Clinics of Canada (www.musiciansclinics.com).

How then can we ensure that loud music is indeed heard through hearing aids or cochlear implants as loud, but not too loud? And how can we ensure that softer sounds are heard as soft, but not too soft?

In order to partially improve this problem—ensuring that sounds are loud enough, but not too loud—hearing aids and cochlear implants use a system called "compression." This is not new to the hearing aid industry. Compression has been used with hearing aids and in radio and television since their onset. Compression essentially means that soft sounds are automatically made louder and loud sounds are automatically made softer. Compression is sometimes called 'automatic volume control" or "automatic gain control." Virtually all hearing aids and cochlear implants use some form of compression. According to research, while there are subtle differences between speech and music, the compression circuit that is set up for speech is actually also quite good for listening to and playing music.

A major difference however, between speech and music is that music is much louder than speech. The loudest shouted speech is typically less than 85 dB, and this is mostly for the vowels such as 'a' in the word 'father'. A level of 85 dB is about the loudness of a dial tone on a telephone, and while we would not like to listen to this for every moment of the day, it's not too loud. In contrast, even very quiet music (classical, jazz, or even soft rock) is well in excess of 85 dB. It's not unusual to listen to your favorite song at 100 dB or even higher.

## The Limits of Modern Hearing Aids and Cochlear Implants

All hearing aids and cochlear implants are similar in the sense that they all have microphones, amplifiers, and some way to transmit that amplified signal to the ear. In hearing aids, the amplified signal is sent to a small loudspeaker (called a receiver) that either sits in the ear or is joined to the ear by an earmold, if the person is wearing a behind the ear hearing aid. In a cochlear implant, the amplified signal is transmitted through the skin to a small array of electrodes that have been surgically implanted in the inner ear. In both cases, sound enters the hearing aid or cochlear implant, is made louder in a manner specific to the needs of the individual, and is then sent to the ear.

The microphone is a wonderful device that has been around since the later part of the 19th century. Like many inventions it has gone through a gradual evolution. Microphones are devices that convert sound (or music) to electrical impulses that can later be amplified. Modern hearing aid and cochlear implant microphones are very sensitive and can transmit sounds as quiet as several decibels, and also can reliably transmit sounds as intense as 115 dB. A level of 115 dB is actually quite loud and typically heard as the louder parts of rock concerts or symphonies. Since the loudest parts of speech is much less than 115 dB (and is typically less than 85 dB) speech through a microphone poses no problem. However, very loud music can sometimes overdrive the microphone causing distortion with a resulting fuzzy sound. In the vast majority of cases however, music and speech can reliably be transmitted through a modern microphone with no ill effects.

Almost all modern hearing aids are "digital." This means that after the microphone but before the amplifier, sound energy is chopped up into tiny portions and each one is assigned a value depending on how loud each portion is. These values are stored as a number in a computer (inside the hearing aid or cochlear implant). This process is called "Analog to Digital conversion" or simply A/D conversion, and is much like slicing a loaf of bread and dealing with each slice individually (see Figure 2-2). An A/D converter is very small and has no trouble fitting into even the smallest hearing aid or cochlear implant shell. The output of the A/D converter goes to the amplifier and this makes each of the millions of stored numbers in the computer louder (or softer) depending on the needs of the individual. Finally, this altered string of numbers is fed into a "Digital to Analog converter" (D/A converter) and sound (if a hearing aid) or an electrical signal (if a cochlear implant) is directed to the ear. In other words, we need to put the modified sliced bread back together again before we send it onto the ear.

Most hearing aid and cochlear implant engineers design these devices to prevent louder sounds from getting to the A/D converter (just after the microphone). There are two reasons for this. The first is that even though the microphones can transmit sounds up to 115 dB reliably, the A/D converter

Figure 2-2: In the Analog-to-Digital (A/D) conversion process with digital hearing aids, sound is chopped up into many pieces (or slices of bread). Used with permission, Musicians' Clinics of Canada (www.musiciansclinics.com).

cannot handle sounds this loud. Usually a clipper (which is like a low-hanging ceiling) is installed that prevents sounds over about 95 dB from entering the hearing aid or cochlear implant. This prevents overdriving the A/D converter and seeks to minimize distortion. This limitation of a 95 dB ceiling has no ill effects on speech, but can have dramatic negative effects for music.

Recall that the loudest sound of speech is about 85 dB and since 85 dB is less than the 95 dB limit that many hearing aids and cochlear implants use, it's like safely going under a bridge—85 dB is less than 95 dB. It is convenient to think of this clipper or ceiling as a low hanging bridge and you are sailing under the bridge in a sail boat with a tall mast. If the bridge is too low (or your mast is too high) trouble will occur. Speech has a "short mast" but music (which is characteristically higher than 95 dB) has a "tall mast." Speech can get through the hearing aid but music unfortunately will not be allowed to get past the A/D converter bridge without distortion.

The second reason is historical. Many hearing aid design engineers set this bridge (even before hearing aids and cochlear implants were digital) at such a low level because they were mostly concerned about speech, which is inherently quieter than music. Shouted speech simply cannot reach the level of the bridge. Perhaps because of the demands of the baby boomer generation, non-speech sounds such as music are quite rightly, becoming more important. And it's these louder music sounds that are distorted at the very beginning of the hearing aid or cochlear implant amplification stages. Once music is distorted, there is no fancy programming or circuitry that can undo the distortion. The distortion of loud music needs to be addressed before it occurs.

## Five Strategies for Hearing Music

The simplest and one of the most effective strategies to improve the clarity and fidelity when listening to music is to turn down the volume of your stereo or MP-3 player (see Figure 2-3 on page 10). This allows the music to get in to the hearing aid or cochlear implant without its mast being chopped off by a low hanging bridge. The listener may still need to turn up the volume later on (after the sound has gotten under the bridge) in order to re-establish the desired loudness of the music.

Figure 2-3: Because modern digital hearing aids and cochlear implants cannot handle overly loud inputs, the best strategy is to turn down the volume of the stereo or MP-3 player and turn up the volume of the hearing aid or cochlear implant (if necessary), not the other way around. Used with permission, Musicians' Clinics of Canada (www.musiciansclinics.com).

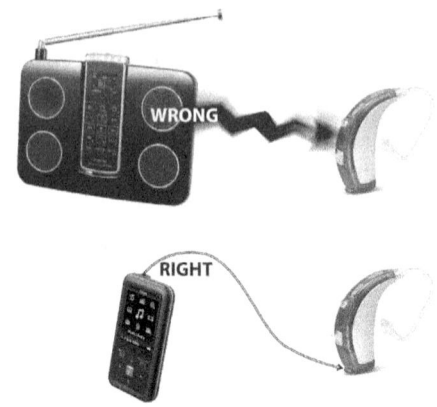

Another modification to the way people listen to or play music is to use an assistive listening device such as an FM system. As the name suggests, an FM system transmits the music (or speech) using an FM radio signal. And like a radio, we need a transmitter and a receiver. The transmitter is a device shaped like a small box with a microphone and is usually situated near the loudspeaker, or the person speaking. Regardless of how far the music or the person speaking is away from the listener, the sound is always received at a sufficiently loud level. This is where the receiver comes in. The FM receiver is a small box (much like the transmitter) but can be either connected to the hearing aid or cochlear implant directly, or be used without a hearing aid. Your hearing health care professional such as your audiologist can assist you with the setting up of such a device. Typically, but not always, the music that you receive from this FM system is at a quieter level so the hearing aid or cochlear implant will not be overdriven. The speech and the music will be clearer with better overall fidelity.

Another option is to discuss with your audiologist about a hearing aid that can handle louder music. The level of exactly what the limiter ceiling is, or the "height of the bridge," is not something that would routinely be stated on the specification sheet for any particular hearing aid. It should be, but according to current hearing aid standards, this is an optional piece of data. The audiologist has several options—one is to contact the hearing aid manufacturer of the hearing aid that has been specified for your hearing loss, and the second is to have the audiologist determine that for themselves. This may sound complicated, but it is not. Perhaps the best strategy is simply to ask the audiologist to perform the following test using the standard equipment available in any audiologist's office: Using a hearing aid test box, set the hearing aid to have 10 dB of gain, and at least 120 dB of output. Then use a 90 dB input to calculate the distortion at 1600 Hz. This may sound complicated but all that we are really doing is testing whether the limiter ceiling or bridge height of the hearing aid is too low for louder music. If there is any appreciable distortion measured then the sail boat mast is being distorted by the bridge. Some hearing aids have a much higher limiter ceiling level than others—these would be better to handle louder music.

A "low tech" solution would be to fool the hearing aid microphone into thinking that it is less sensitive than it really is. Placing a piece of tape over the microphone opening for example, would decrease its sensitivity, thereby providing more head room—the bridge has effectively been moved up while the tape is covering the microphone. This temporary change can be used whenever one wants to listen to or play louder music.

For those people who have behind the ear hearing aids with directional microphones, another "trick" may be helpful.

Directional microphones are found in almost all behind the ear hearing aids and many smaller custom made ones. These microphones are designed to suppress noise if it is coming from the rear direction. Directional microphones, in combination with a binaural fitting (i.e., two hearing aids), and the use of an assistive listening device (such as an FM system) would optimize many hearing aid fittings, especially in noisier situations. The "trick" involves turning the behind the ear hearing aid around—the earmold will still fit nicely into the ear, but the tubing in the earhook has been twisted 180 degrees around such that the front of the hearing aid faces to the rear. This is especially fine if you have long hair, where nobody can see how the hearing aid is fitting. This works because the ports of the directional microphone in the hearing aid will be reversed such that sound from the front will be suppressed—this will fool the hearing aid microphone that receives the louder music to be less sensitive—again with the effect of raising the limiter bridge.

CHAPTER 3

# Hearing Protection for Musicians

*Marshall Chasin, AuD., M.Sc., Aud(C), Reg. CASLPO*

## Introduction

Music, like speech, has energy over much of the range of the piano keyboard. Low frequency fundamental energy can be found for the bass notes on the left side of the keyboard and harmonics and higher frequency notes can be found on the right side. This is true of most musical instruments. Ideally, the best form of hearing protection would be to simply reach up and turn down the volume control knob such that all sounds are turned down equally. The relationship between the lower frequency fundamental energy and its higher frequency harmonics would be maintained. However, this ideal scenario cannot be achieved with standard hearing protection that was designed for the factory worker.

All hearing protection, including normal, industrial strength hearing protection has to follow the laws of physics. We all know that the acoustic impedance of the acoustic inertance is proportional to frequency. Well, we don't really know that, but we can understand the English translation—high frequencies don't like small spaces or obstructions.

When a piano is played in a room and someone listens to it in the next room, the longer wavelength low frequency sounds go through the wall almost unaffected. However, the higher frequency fundamental notes and harmonics on the right hand side of the piano keyboard are obstructed and attenuated by the wall. People in the next room hear the left side of the piano keyboard, but the right side is reduced in intensity. Unless something special is done for hearing protection or the walls in a room, the effect is that the balance of music (and speech) will be severely altered—low frequencies can still be heard well, but not the higher frequency energy of music or the higher frequency consonant sounds in speech. The consonants give speech understanding.

With conventional hearing protection music (and speech) will sound hollow, distant, and in the case of speech, unintelligible. What then can be done? Short of appealing the ubiquitous law of physics—high frequencies do not like small spaces or obstructions—there have been some ingenious approaches around this problem.

The most successful approach was introduced in 1988 by a company called Etymotic Research (www.etymotic.com). This book is not about any one manufacturer of products but this is a case where the world leader was, and still is, this one company. Based on some earlier research by an engineer named Elmer Carlson, Etymotic Research came out with a custom earplug called the ER-15 (with the ER standing for Etymotic Research and the '15' being the amount in decibels that it attenuated or reduced all sounds equally by). The ER-15 takes advantage of some well known acoustic principles and in its design boosts many of the higher frequencies that would normally be lost to the listener. This essentially acts like a hand break against the earplug from cutting out too much of the higher frequency sounds. The net effect is a flat or uniform earplug attenuator that reduces all sounds (both the right and the left hand sides of the piano keyboard) by exactly 15 decibels. With this form of hearing protection, the bass still sounds like the bass, the trumpet still sounds like the trumpet and the piccolo (unfortunately) still sounds like the piccolo.

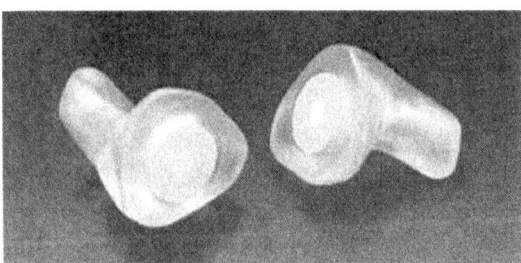

Figure 3-1: A pair of ER-15 uniform attenuator custom made earplugs that provide exactly 15 decibels of hearing protection without altering the sound of the music. Figure courtesy of Etymotic Research. Used with permission.

## Sound is Dropped by Exactly 15 Decibels

At first sight, this does not sound like a lot and indeed clinically when I see musicians who are being fit with a pair of ER-15 earplugs, they do comment "is this all?" When it comes to hearing protection, more is not necessarily better. Fifteen decibels of hearing protection is actually quite enough for the vast majority of musicians and those who like to listen to music. The decibel is a rather complex measure of the intensity of the sound. It involves logarithms and reference points, but the bottom line is that a mere 3 decibel reduction in sound (which is almost not even noticeable) would cut the potential damage from loud music (or noise) in half. Another 3 dB reduction would reduce it one quarter; another 3 dB reduction (we're now down to 9 dB in total) would reduce it to one eighth; another 3 dB to 1/16; and finally another reduction of 3 dB to 15 dB overall, would reduce the potential damage from music (or noise) to 1/32. This means that a 15 dB reduction in sound would allow a person to be in a loud musical environment for 32 times as long without damage to their hearing, as a person who was not wearing any hearing protection.

The logistics of obtaining a pair of ER-15 custom made earplugs is to make an appointment to see an audiologist. Other than having your hearing assessed, they can make custom earmold impressions of your ears and will send that to a local earmold laboratory. This would be the same laboratory that makes earmolds for hearing aids. About a week or two later the custom made ER-15 is ready to be fit. The material of the mold is flesh colored and typically made of medical-grade silicon. Ideally when fit, musicians will forget that there is anything in their ears and music will sound like it was without hearing protection but now listening will be safe.

By 1992 it became apparent that percussionists occasionally required slightly more hearing protection than the ER-15 and the ER-25 was created. As the name suggests, this provides 25 decibels of hearing protection which is identical for all sounds. Without wading through the math, a typical drummer would be able to play his or her instrument about 256 times as long before the same damage occurs as a drummer who was not wearing hearing protection.

Not everyone wants a pair of custom made earplugs (at a cost of $200) so the ER-20 was invented. This one-size-fits-all earplug, provides hearing protection that is somewhere between the ER-15 and the ER-25, but sells for a fraction of the cost of the custom made earplugs. The ER-20 has recently been re-named ETY•plugs and is shown is figure 3-2. These actually come in a range of colors and several different sizes.

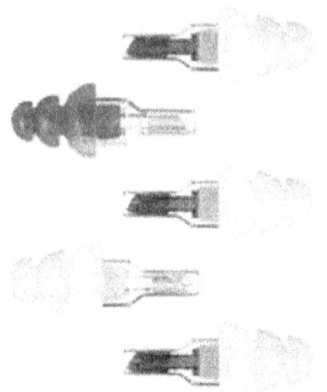

Figure 3-2: The ETY•plugs which are non-custom and one-size-fits-all. Because one size does not really fit all, the ETY•plugs come in different sizes. Figure courtesy of Etymotic Research. Used with permission.

Other manufacturers have recently come out with similar devices—hearing protection that is uniform or flat and treats all of the sounds similarly, and information on these can be obtained from your local audiologist. Some look similar to the ER-15 while others are unusual shaped headsets that have bunny eared "side resonators."

### Hearing Aids and Hearing Protection

Can my hearing aids act as hearing protection, or since I already have a hearing loss do I still need hearing protection? The answer is yes, and yes. Although it is not straightforward, research performed in the 1990s did show that a person with a hearing loss is no more, no less susceptible to further music or noise induced hearing loss than someone with normal or near normal hearing. Hearing protection is important for everyone.

Depending on the exact nature of your hearing aids, they may be protective. Some can be set to provide "negative amplification" or hearing protection if the sound in the room is too loud. This may differ from hearing aid to hearing aid, and from one hearing aid fitting to another. It is best to consult your audiologist for more information with your specific hearing aid fitting. And what about the earmold—the piece that joins the behind-the-ear hearing aid to the ear? If there is no air hole or "vent" in the earmold, then this can function quite well as an earplug. If there is a sizable vent in the earmold, this will limit the usefulness of your hearing aid as a hearing protector. Again, it's best to consult with your audiologist about this issue.

# CHAPTER 4

# Personal Stories and Strategies

*Members of the Association of Adult Musicians*
*with Hearing Loss (AAMHL)*

**Jennifer Castellano**—Pianist and composer
*Thornwood, New York*

I was born both visually and hearing impaired; however, my hearing impairment was not officially diagnosed until I was eight years old. Strangely though, I didn't learn how to talk until I was three and a half years old. I think my family thought that I was just a late bloomer. After all, I didn't learn how to walk until I was two. Also, they were focused on helping me overcome my visual challenges.

I have a "cookie bite" hearing loss. That is, I can hear high and low frequencies better than the middle frequencies. Because I was able to hear high and low frequencies in both ears, it was thought that my hearing was okay.

I didn't decide to take piano lessons until an "incident" occurred at a friend's house when I was about seven years old. My childhood friend showed me a small electronic keyboard that had a series of buttons at the top. She pushed one button and soon I heard a simple melody with a drum accompaniment. I listened to it a couple times. Then she pushed another button which produced the drum accompaniment alone. My fingers immediately jumped to the keyboard and I began playing the song exactly how I remembered it. My friend immediately jumped up and ran into the kitchen where her mother was. I followed to see what the excitement was all about. "Mom! Mom!" she cried "She can play it!" I was shocked by her enthusiastic response. I had no idea what the big deal was. Wasn't that how everyone learned music? My friend's mother told me that I should take piano lessons.

I began studying piano when I was eight years old. I had my first piano lesson on March 1, 1990. It was a Thursday and I remember it fairly well.

In a matter of minutes I had mastered where all the notes on the keyboard were (including sharps and flats). This was the first time I learned all their names. My teacher immediately noticed that I had a very good memory. A few weeks later she later discovered that I had perfect pitch.

A few months after beginning my piano studies, I learned something about myself that would greatly influence my philosophy of hearing music. In May 1990 I learned that I had a hearing loss and that I needed to wear hearing aids. This came as a shock to me. I didn't know anyone my age who had a hearing impairment or who wore hearing aids. The only person I knew who had a hearing loss and wore hearing aids was my paternal grandmother, but her hearing loss was the result of aging. So when I was told that I needed a hearing aid, my first reaction was something like: "What? And skip middle age?"

It seemed like a paradox to be a hearing impaired musician who had perfect pitch. On one hand, I was told that I had such a good musical ear, but on the other I was told that I was deaf as a door nail. Answering the telephone was a big fear of mine as a child because it was always difficult for me to hear the person on the other end.

I was 12 years old before I began to accept my hearing loss. Not only did I accept it, I never allowed it to prevent me from continuing my musical studies. In May 2004, I earned a Bachelor of Arts in Music at Manhattanville College where I concentrated in piano performance. In May 2008 I completed a Master of Music at Purchase College where I concentrated in composition.

I didn't begin composing until I was in college and began studying music theory and composition with Mary Ann Joyce-Walter. Her original works inspired me to begin composing my own music. Dr. Joyce was my very first teacher of composition who continues to be one of my biggest musical supporters and closest friends.

When writing music, I usually hear rhythm before melody. I do hear melodies but the first thing I take notice of is rhythm and meter. Rhythm is what makes my music tick. Not only can you hear rhythm but you can feel it. I remember the choral director from college commenting on a rhythmic passage in one of our songs: "I shouldn't hear any feet tapping. Rhythm is felt from within." I couldn't agree more.

My biggest challenges in music are related to both my vision and hearing. With my vision it was fairly obvious. I had difficulty seeing the music.

My scores always had to be and continue to be enlarged to a readable size. For the last five years, I have been wearing a telescopic lens so I can read the score while sitting at a regular distance from the piano.

Aural challenges are a little less obvious. I have been wearing hearing aids since I was eight years old. While I can hear some sounds without them (like the high pitched calls of my two small parrots, Sunny and Nikki), I wear them all the time. They help make the sounds louder and clearer. I find the use of an FM system extremely helpful when playing chamber and ensemble music. When playing in my church's handbell choir, the director always wears my FM transmitter at rehearsals so that I can understand her better.

In general, I can hear and recognize individual pitches and chords; however, when it comes to a piano's tone quality and touch, that is Greek to me. I could never tell if I was producing a nice sound or not. I could just hear loud and soft. I would spend a long time trying to figure out if the phrase "moved" in the right way or if the melody could be heard above the accompaniment. I can never hear the balance between the hands. When I was in college, a lot of my jury comments stated that I produced a harsh tone. This always confused me. What did a harsh tone sound like compared to a nice one? Even today I sometimes find it hard to tell the difference when I listen to other pianists play.

My senses were only able to do so much for me. It wasn't until I started my piano studies with Flora Kuan that things started to make more sense. I don't know if anyone ever told her that her teaching methods are a gift to the hearing impaired, but I would have to say this statement holds true. Since we began working together, I now play with more ease and confidence.

Dr. Kuan would not describe how a passage should sound by only using aural or visual words. She would often use words that related to touch and feeling. "It should feel gummy and sticky," she would say in reference to a legato passage. With regard to tone quality she would say something like: "You cannot produce a nice sound when your hand is hard. It has to be soft, the wrist cannot be tight. It has to be loose." Or when referring to a passage that required a strong yet mellow tone she would say something like: "You have to cushion the sound. Move your wrists down slowly but firmly." Now I was beginning to understand. I may not have been able to hear an extreme difference but I could feel it and that is how I knew if I was producing a better sound.

I truly learned the real art of listening. It goes far beyond the human ear. Over time, I learned to pay attention to how sound traveled through parts of my body: my finger tips, hands, wrists, arms and even my shoulders and back.

One of the most memorable things that Dr. Kuan ever said to me was that "music is for everybody." It was amazing to hear something like that come from an accomplished musician, but I agree with her. Music is not about being the best, but about giving your best. It isn't about how much ability you have, but how you use the abilities you have. Like the American author, educator and clergyman, Henry Van Dyke, once said: "Use what talents you possess: the woods would be very silent if no birds sang there except those that sang best."

## Wendy Cheng—Viola student
*Gaithersburg, Maryland*

My hearing loss was first diagnosed at the age of nine. My parents believe ototoxic medications taken when I was two years old caused my hearing loss. At the time of diagnosis, the right ear was found to have a profound hearing loss and the left ear had a mild to moderate loss. Over the years, the left ear slowly deteriorated, and then settled down at 70 dB across all frequency ranges. I wore a Phonic Ear behind-the-ear hearing aid in my left ear for many years. In March 1996 I had a viral infection and lost what was left of my hearing. I decided to get a cochlear implant and in January 1997 received a Clarion 1.2 implant in my right ear, which has since been replaced with a new Harmony cochlear implant in 2010. In February 2008 I decided to go bilateral and received a Harmony cochlear implant from Advanced Bionics in my left ear.

My mother encouraged my sisters and I to study classical piano, so I had piano lessons from the age of seven to 15. In high school, I fell in love with the sound of the violin but because of my severe hearing loss, no one in my family gave me much chance of success with this instrument (since the intonation requirements for this instrument is so much higher than the piano). I finally began violin lessons at the age of 19 as a college sophomore, and haven't stopped since. I've participated in string quartets, string and full orchestra workshops. I switched over from violin to viola when I realized I did not hear tones above third position on the violin's E string very well.

There are several strategies I have used over the years to integrate my hearing loss into my music studies. The first and foremost is using an assistive listening device (ALD). The idea is to have the music teacher or the conductor wear the transmitter unit while I wear the receiver unit. This resolves the thorny issue of needing to lipread the teacher while getting instructions on playing an instrument (you're expected to be looking at the instrument instead of the teacher's face). So far I have found Comtek's AT-216 FM system and Etymotic Research's Companion Mic system to work the best during my music lessons. I also use the Companion Mic system when playing string quartets with my daughters and nephew. I have the violinists in the group wear the Companion Mic transmitters and this really helps to ensure that I can hear the other players and not get lost as often as before.

Some other strategies I use involve ways to get around the high intonation requirements of learning to play an unfretted bowed string instrument, especially since my viola does not give strong vibrations and not all notes have ringing tones to help me determine whether I am playing in tune or not. One device I use a great deal in my viola studies is to use a visual tuner like the Korg OT-120 to develop spatial memory. I also put black duct tape over a note that is just too hard for me to play in tune. Last but not least, I have also entertained the idea of studying a fretted bowed string instrument like the viola da gamba or take up the harp, but these are just ideas at the moment.

Due to time constraints, I am unable to participate in community orchestras at this point in my life. However, I have also found a satisfying way to keep up with my ensemble skills by participating in the advanced handbell choir at my Catholic parish. The music director wears the Companion Mic system transmitter and it is so wonderful to be able to hear her instructions coming through my implants without having to lipread her.

Having spent the last twenty years developing my skills as an amateur string player, I am eagerly looking forward to seeing where the next twenty years will take me. Someday, I hope to pursue my interest and love of music full-time and obtain a degree in music.

**Joan Ernst**—Music educator and choral director
*Hertford, North Carolina*

I was born with perfect hearing into a very musical family. Classical music was always playing in our home and our whole family sang in our church choir. I started studying piano at the age of six, cello at the age of nine and voice at the age of 16. I attended the Eastman School of Music, University of Rochester (NY) from 1963-1967 as a voice major. In 1973 I received my Masters in Music Ed. from C.W. Post College, Long Island University (NY), with voice as my primary instrument. That same year I started my 30-year teaching career in South Huntington Public Schools in New York state. In addition to teaching, I continued to be a soprano soloist in our church choir and community chorus.

My hearing was perfect throughout my college years and the first 10 years of my teaching career. By the time I was in my late 30s, I became aware that I was missing words in conversations—asking "What?" too often. In addition, I noticed that I was hearing some high musical pitches sharp. I first noticed that the treble stops on the organ seemed too high. (An octave seemed more like a minor 9th). Then it started affecting my own singing and my family and fellow choir members noticed I was going sharp occasionally.

By the age of 38 (1983) I had my first hearing aids and an early mid-life crisis! The aids were analog at that time, and were fitted solely for speech. So while the amplification did help me some with conversation it did not improve music. Plus, audiologists really did not understand what I was going through as I tried to describe what I was hearing. My whole life was music! How could this be happening?

As my hearing continued to gradually deteriorate, music became more and more out-of-tune. Eventually I had to stop singing all together, which was devastating. But our church choir director utilized me as an accompanist and assistant conductor at times so I could continue to be musically active in church.

Teaching became more challenging as I tried to cope but keep my hearing problem secret. (Of course I wore my hair long so no one saw the aids). Finally, I had to confide in a few trusted colleagues. At this point I was teaching K-6 general music classes, chorus, string lessons and orchestra. One fellow music teacher was extremely helpful by coming to chorus and orchestra dress rehearsals before our concerts and listening for balance and pitch problems. He also helped tune the string instruments in my orchestra before concerts.

But the time came when I had to tell my supervisor the problem and ask for an assignment that did not require me to prepare performance groups. Thanks to the ADA (Americans with Disabilities Act), I was not worried about being fired. I was assigned to a K-2 school and had student teachers over the last five years of my career. This was a terrific boost for me because the student teachers were not only able to assume the singing and hearing parts of the job, but they also affirmed for me that I had a great deal to give from my years of experience. Instead of being focused on what I could no longer do, I was aware of what I still could do. My student teachers energized me and made my last few years so much more enjoyable.

My husband and our two daughters have been equally involved in music avocationally and we were often attending concerts when our daughters performed. At these concerts, our daughters would always supply me with copies of the music they were singing so I could follow along. This greatly helped my level of enjoyment and understanding.

Yet, when I retired from teaching in 2002 I had no intention of being active in music again. Somehow I thought I could purge my life of music. We moved to a small town in northeastern North Carolina and joined an Episcopal church that had a small choir and no director. When they heard my husband's wonderful tenor voice, they pressed him into service. Soon he told them about my background and I was invited to direct the choir for Christmas services. That was seven years ago and I am still the choir director.

The choir has grown and the feedback I receive is extremely encouraging. When I am directing, I am reading the music and know what it should sound like. I try to convey that in my directing and it seems to work. The choir members know of my limitations and work with me. Through lip reading and body language, I can perceive what is happening and notice mistakes—especially rhythmic ones. But I cannot tell if someone sings the wrong note at the right time. They are on the honor system to tell me if they are not getting the right notes. My husband, who has an excellent ear for music, sings tenor from the back row and often gives me visual cues when someone is off.

Over the last 20 years I have chased the improving technology going from analog to digital aids; my husband installed an induction loop system in our car and in our kitchen; I used a Phonak personal FM system with my Widex Senso Diva aids at parties and in restaurants; and I used a Bluetooth streamer with my newer Epoq hearing aids. I have used TV ears, closed captioning and a captioned telephone. Each of these new devices helped some with conversation, but did nothing for music.

Finally, despite all the bells and whistles, my speech discrimination scores were so poor that I qualified for a cochlear implant. In April 2009 I received an Advanced Bionics cochlear implant at Duke University. The difference in my speech discrimination is astounding. With my CI I now use the telephone like a normal-hearing person. I can now use a cell phone and I gave my captioned phone away. I can attend movies again and understand TV without the captioning, if necessary.

But, music has not improved. My pitch discrimination is still very poor. Like hearing aids, cochlear implants are geared toward speech and the research for music perception with cochlear implants is still very new. Now instead of chasing technology I am chasing the research. I check the internet for places where subjects are needed for projects testing music perception with CIs. I also use the music rehab program available online from the Advanced Bionics website.

At this point, the most important coping skill I have is to focus on the improved quality of life I am experiencing with the CI and share experiences and stories with those who understand.

## Mike McConnell—Ragtime pianist
*Battle Ground, Washington*

I was born with hearing loss when my mother contracted the German measles or rubella while I was still in the womb. This occurred during the rubella outbreak of the northwest during the 1960s. While I was born with profound hearing loss in my left ear, my right ear was somewhat spared with a hearing loss of about 70 dB. At age three I was fitted with a hearing aid in my better ear.

My fascination with music began at the early age of seven. I begged my mom and dad to get a piano so I could learn how to play. I continued to practice on the family piano while growing up though my sister and brother chose not to. I enjoyed performing in piano recitals though I didn't take much stock in the fact that I was a hard of hearing kid who could play the piano and probably stood out from the rest of the people there.

At about age 11 my first piece was a simplified version of "The Entertainer"—a widely popular and recognizable Scott Joplin ragtime piece. And during my early teen years I rediscovered ragtime as my piano skills progressed to playing more complicated and original ragtime piano pieces such as "Maple Leaf Rag," "The Entertainer," "The Cascades," and "Original Rags." I was hooked on this intoxicating music.

Most of my life has been a rather musical one. I can play any instrument that I want to since I am able to hear all range of musical notes with the help of my hearing aid. I have played the violin, taught myself to play the saxophone to the point of being good enough to play in a middle school band, and played the drums and xylophone in middle and high school bands. I was the bass drummer in my high school band and we competed in marching band competitions in Georgia, South Carolina, and Florida. My hearing aids helped me to hear the complete range of most of the musical instruments I wanted to play. In marching band, the conductor helps in keeping with the beat. Everybody looks at the conductor whenever they face him/her. Keeping in step with the music helped me keep up with the beat and following the beat of the other drummers helped me know when it was my turn to play.

Although I have learned to play several instruments, my main musical instrument and first love has always been the piano. As a student at Gallaudet University, I played "Maple Leaf Rag" on stage for an audience.

My love for the piano stayed with me even though I did not have much opportunity to play during my days in college because of family obligations and getting an education. Even when I occasionally had time to practice, it was never enough. In that absence I read books on ragtime and the people who played ragtime, and collected ragtime piano sheet music whenever I could. What was a big help during graduate school at University of Idaho was the availability of pianos on campus and the famous Lionel Hampton International Jazz Festival held annually on campus. Over the last several years the internet has made it easier for me to learn and experience more about ragtime, the people (new and old), the history, and the music through YouTube. It has given me blogging opportunities, allowed me to become involved in a ragtime discussion forum and provided a way to download lots of free ragtime music sheets dating back to the early 1890s.

The time finally came in December 2008 when I decided it was time to buy myself a new piano and not have a broken down piano to worry about. I decided upon a goal to get back into ragtime with fervor and become the first known deaf ragtime pianist. It will take some time, gradually and slowly for sure, as I branch into other well known ragtime composers such as W.R. McKanlass, Charles Leslie Johnson, George Botsford, Holmes Travis, and many other well known and not so well known composers, including the early jazz pieces by Jelly Roll Morton.

Over time I was finally able to get to the point of practicing four or five hours a day if I wanted to. Though my ideal amount of time is about two to three hours a day, the challenge is finding the time to play when my kids are not around. It will take some time to get all of my piano coordination and skill back on track. I may be a "natural" in some sense, but it sure doesn't feel like it. There is a 25-year gap I've got to catch up on. My sight reading is getting easier nowadays whenever I come across a new ragtime music sheet piece, though by no means can I whiz right though them, yet. There are thousands of ragtime sheets out there, many of them available over the internet. I collect them for my growing ragtime portfolio, both in electronic format and hard copy. My goal is to play as many of these ragtime pieces and memorize some of them when I can. Someday I'll eventually move into early jazz pieces (e.g. Jelly Roll Morton) and stride piano (e.g. Fats Waller) but for now it's all ragtime and a lot of catching up to do.

My challenge nowadays is to find other ragtime pianists that I could associate myself with and keep my interest high on playing the piano on a daily/regular basis. When I moved to Washington in June of 2009 from New Mexico, I learned about the Portland Ragtime Society group in Portland, Oregon, which turned out to be a 45-minute drive from my house. This group meets and plays ragtime together once a month at a public eatery that supports a piano. Currently we play at the Elevated Coffee in Portland.

Other challenges include the continuing documentation of my progress in my Ragtime Piano! blog (http://ragtimepiano.blogspot.com/). I am always on the lookout for deaf or hard of hearing pianists. And when I do find one I try learn about the person and document that in my blog. I plan to include more videos for my blog and on my YouTube channel, interviews on ragtime pianists, and anything else I can do to increase my focus and interest on ragtime and piano playing. The internet is a big help and a valuable source of my continued learning. There are lots of strategies I can offer to help and inspire others in playing the piano and ragtime music. At the very least, we will have fun getting there!

## Erin McKenzie-Christensen—Violist
*Adelaide, Australia*

I am 28 years old and live in Adelaide, Australia. I began playing viola in 1998 and still continue taking lessons. I occasionally play the violin and have sung in the Adelaide University Choral Society since 2000. I was also involved with the Tutti Ensemble in 2008 and various other orchestras and choirs prior to July 2008. I also used to play the piano, taking lessons from 1994-2000.

My journey of music and disability first started in 2006 when I became partially deaf with no hearing in one ear and some in the other. As a string player I think most people would have given up at this point or changed instruments. I am glad I did not but I had to find a way to continue playing the instruments I loved. I already had chronic pain and some fatigue but these were somewhat overcome because I wanted to be involved with music so much. I had to wait until my Disability Support Pension was approved to get hearing aids since we could not afford them.

While waiting almost a year for hearing aids, Hearing Solutions showed me several devices that could help me hear in addition to using head-phones. I fell in love with an FM system which consists of a receiver and a transmitter. The transmitter has a microphone which picks up the sound from the TV, a person, viola or choir and then sends it wirelessly to the re-ceiver, which sends the sound to my hearing aid through the telecoil program and induction loop. Hearing Solutions let me borrow the equipment to see if it would help me in hearing my viola. It not only helped me hear the viola but also the TV, my husband, CDs, etc. It was wonderful. At my lesson my teacher was impressed with how much it helped with my intonation. I was more confident and honestly I didn't feel like a beginner anymore.

Of course this experience was short-lived because I was only borrowing it. I had to find a more permanent solution. Unfortunately, these devices are quite expensive. Since early 2007 while studying at TAFE, a tertiary institution in Australia, I have been fortunate to borrow the FM system from them to use in my studies. Using the system every day for several hours has helped to solve some of my hearing difficulties, playing the vi-ola, and singing too. Placed in front of the choir near my section, it picks up the sound or I give the transmitter to a person in the choir and they sing into it. I use the FM system with my hearing aids now. My hearing deteriorated further during 2008 and I can no longer hear through headphones anymore.

The other helpful thing for me in mixing music and hearing loss has been my supportive viola teacher. Seriously, I went to my viola lesson one day and asked her, "Do you think I will be able to continue music?" and she replied, "Unless there is a medical reason, I can't see why not!" She has been so helpful and supportive ever since.

Some of the challenges and frustrations I have faced with integrating my hearing loss into my musical activities include finding ways to continue making music. If I hadn't found out about an FM system in the first place and been given an opportunity to try it with my instrument or in choir, I never would have known this would work. Another challenge is helping choral and orchestral musicians understand that people with hearing loss can still be musicians.

**Cherisse Miller**—Pianist, organist and piano teacher
*Columbia, South Carolina*

Music has always been a major part of my life since the day I was born to parents who were professional musicians. Practicing, going to concerts, and singing in church—music was all around me. Today, I too am a professional musician—only I have a binaural sensorineural hearing loss. I teach piano in my studio at home, I am a church organist in a large Baptist church, and I enjoy accompanying choirs, vocalists, instrumentalists, and collaborating with other musicians and pedagogues throughout the state and community. I recently earned a Master of Music in Piano Performance in 2005 and a Doctor of Musical Arts in Piano Pedagogy in 2009 from the University of South Carolina. I love what I do despite my hearing loss and accept the challenges and frustrations as a musician with hearing loss as who I am and try to make the best of it.

I only discovered the nature of my hearing loss by pure luck and my inquisitive nature during a rare visit to the ENT office about 25 years ago. Until then, my parents thought my hearing loss was hereditary and were unaware of how or when my hearing loss occurred, which I naturally accepted. I was told by this "new" doctor, after reviewing records from old hearing tests from elementary school, that my hearing was normal prior to 1962. He then suspected that something happened to me in 1962. That "something" was pneumonia when I was eight years old. Further investigation from medical records and with my pharmacist confirmed Chloramycetin as the probable cause.

My most recent audiogram in January 2010 showed a 10-20 dB loss over the past four years. I have poor speech discrimination scores of 60% in both ears. Hearing loss in my "good" left ear is mild to moderately severe sloping to profound and my right ear is moderately severe sloping to profound. I was fitted with the new Widex Mind hearing aids in early 2010.

My story begins with sharing personal experiences over the past 45 years as a piano teacher, church musician, and graduate student with progressive hearing loss. Despite my hearing loss, I never questioned that hearing loss would keep me from making music or teaching music. I learned to speak, acquired a basic vocabulary, became familiar with everyday sounds and was already playing the piano before my hearing loss became severe. My love of music was already in my heart long before I knew or understood my hearing loss. My parents reminded me every year on the first day of school to sit at the front of the class, which was always demeaning and embarrassing for me. I am sure I did not always do this, causing my grades and self esteem to suffer. I assume my hearing loss was mild to moderate, since I made it through my senior year in high school in 1970 without hearing aids. I earned a BA in music while wearing one BTE hearing aid and not telling a soul about my hearing loss, which remained a "secret" until twenty years ago. Without realizing, I developed many basic survival techniques for reading lips, watching people's gestures, facial expressions, and any other visual clues that would help me connect words and meaning when I could not hear effectively.

I would evaluate my years of experience using hearing aids as sufficient. I do not recall the quality of sound being that much better each time I got new ones; except for regaining sounds lost when the old aids began losing power. My first experience with digital hearing aids during the mid 1990s was the most frustrating endured in trying a new hearing device, only to finally realize they were not made to hear music. The audiologist worked patiently with me for a couple of months, and I remember thinking I must be her first patient who was a musician. I was very disappointed, since for the first time in my life I could eavesdrop and understand people talking around me, behind me and across the room with clarity and seldom heard consonants. Yet the sounds of music I also wanted to hear were consumed by the same condensers that enabled me to understand speech. While waiting for technology that offered both speech and music, another audiologist introduced me to programmable hearing aids. They did not have the clarity as the digitals, yet offered three different programs: normal speech, the T-switch, and a party/restaurant mode for cutting down on background noise. Only after wearing two hearing aids did I hear a few additional higher pitches on the piano and a gain a better balance between both ears. Only after binaural digital hearing aids did I hear clarity and crisp consonants.

In 1990 after being fitted with an ITE hearing aid in the left ear and used in combination with the BTE in the right ear, I remember playing the eight-foot Yamaha grand piano at my church. I could hear at least 8-10 new pitches in the top two octave range of the keyboard. This was exciting because at one time I actually didn't think anyone could hear the highest pitches on the piano. The organist and I played piano-organ duets every Sunday. Both instruments were fairly new and of excellent quality. The organ amplification was also excellent for the sanctuary. Although we were face to face on opposite sides of the sanctuary, a mini Peavey amp close by allowed me to hear myself as well as hear the speaker from the platform. Fortunately, the organist had great listening capabilities and listened musically. He let me lead in tempos and any fluctuations in tempo. When I got out of sync with him in tempo or playing expressively, he was able to follow my musical leading. This was fortunate for me and I realize that not all situations have this kind of flexibility. In similar situations problems occur in staying together because it is difficult to hear both instruments simultaneously, especially when a partner does not have equal musical abilities or keen listening skills. I cannot hear them well enough above my playing to make the musical adjustments necessary for a unified performance.

Up until 2001 I had never given my hearing loss much thought as to the specifics of my coping skills, strategies, understanding my audiogram, and how hearing loss affected my life as a musician. I have always adapted and tried to do the best I could. Over time as my hearing loss progressed, I gradually began avoiding situations where it would be difficult to hear, unless accompanied by a family member or good friend. In a sense, I created a world where I did not have to be involved with groups of people on a daily or even weekly basis. I taught piano privately, since I could manage one-on-one conversations, played in churches, directed children's choirs, which were difficult at times when I could not understand the children. These part-time activities enabled me to have periods of quiet time during my days to rest my ears, instead of working a full-time job, where I would constantly have to listen. I worked with children's choirs over twenty years ago and would not be able to do that today because of the noise levels and my inability to multitask, all at the same time trying to remember my plans for teaching. I find it very frustrating and difficult to think and talk at the same time when one or more people are talking.

In my work as a piano teacher and church choir accompanist, communication problems usually outweigh any problems of hearing the music. Beginners and intermediate level students for the most part play a 3 to 3 1/2 octave range in the middle of the piano keyboard and sound textures are fairly thin (single or two lines, melody with simple accompaniment). I am quite capable of hearing all of the pitches used in playing this level repertoire. I can match pitches, hear wrong notes away from the piano and tell which key is wrong within a chord. I am very sensitive to pianos being out of tune or performing on an unfamiliar piano with sound and tuning issues when playing from memory (which is not often).

In choir rehearsals, I can identify the voice part singing the wrong notes. I am able to hear when choirs and vocalists sing off pitch. The piano accompaniments are not so difficult or complex for the majority of church choral music that cause any specific problems. As long as I am consistently focused on the director and learn to anticipate his actions, I am competent in doing a good job musically. I always explain my specific needs to a new director prior to rehearsals which are—to speak in my direction and to avoid talking before the choir stops singing. Most everyone I have worked with has been supportive and patient while adapting to my hearing loss. It does become difficult when a director speaks too fast in rehearsals, causing hesitation in my response while processing what I thought he said and finding the correct measure in the music. I am constantly looking for visual cues to help me anticipate his every move.

Serving as the organist in a moderately large Baptist church for 16 years is gradually becoming more difficult as amplified contemporary praise bands are becoming the more accepted musical accompaniment. I no longer participate in contemporary praise band due to the dangerous sound levels and the difficulty of not being able to keep up in following the beat without a traditional music director leading.

Returning to graduate school in 2002 was an endeavor that took me completely outside of my small quiet world of controlled listening to many hours a day of constant music, talking and other environmental noises. I quickly realized the programmable aids were not working for me anymore. My audiologist informed me of the music program now available on the Widex Senso Divas and let me try them over the course of the semester. I doubt that I would have been able to continue past that first semester without these new digital hearing aids. They worked so well and contributed to my self confidence and satisfaction as a teacher, performer, and in my new-found ability of making mostly A's, which was not something I achieved as a teenager.

My piano teacher was eager to learn from me as a hearing impaired student, as his special interests included teaching young students with learning disabilities who were blind and/or autistic. He quickly adapted by not talking while he modeled correct technique at his piano and waited for the sound to decay before talking. As a piano major, my music was much more advanced than what I played at church or taught. I soon realized, as far as sound was concerned, that baroque and classical literature (Bach, Mozart) were not as difficult to hear due to the smaller range of the pianoforte, as some of the romantic music (Chopin, Brahms) and especially the 20th Century piano literature, because of the thicker textures and the extreme use of the upper and lower ranges of the piano. I constantly doubted myself when very low pitches were distorted because of volume and/or overtones, and in the extreme upper register I only heard thuds. I learned to practice small sections of music in a comfortable hearing range to learn the correct sounds and finger memory.

While practicing without my hearing aids one day, I discovered I could hear the clarity and clean, even sounds in my playing from feeling and hearing the action of the keys. All of the resonance that sometimes overlapped was gone, which I believe affected my perception of how I sounded. It was a good way to check my memory, but lacked the warmth and fullness I prefer when listening to myself play the piano with my hearing aids.

Octaves are not as difficult even though I usually do not hear the top note in the upper register, but audiate it from the lower note. I learned to appreciate 20th century music, but found abstract music—when lacking tonality and music with too much dissonance—to be very difficult and even more tedious to learn. I made an effort to work on minimalist John Adam's *China Gates,* with constant repetitious melodic patterns changing on irregular beats. It was hard to spend long periods of time practicing it—even though I did like the music—because repeated key patterns in the upper range produced bell-like oscillating sounds that did not sound like the piano. It was not comfortable to my ears as well.

The seven years I spent as a graduate student were a rewarding musical and personal journey. It was a constant challenge to cultivate new listening skills while adapting to the rigorous schedule of classes, practicing, performing and teaching, not to mention family time. The bad news is—my hearing will continue to get worse. The good news is—new technology will continue to improve. My only hope is my story will offer inspiration and a realization of the growing need for quality sound technology for hearing music through hearing aids for musicians and anyone with hearing loss.

**Renee Blue O'Connell**—Music practitioner, guitarist and singer
*Charlottesville, Virginia*

Many years ago I had a good friend who was studying composition at Northwestern University. He invited me over one night to hear his latest piece on the keyboard. After waiting for what seemed a long time, I finally asked, "When are you going to play me your new song?" He looked stunned and answered, "I just did—didn't you hear it?" I didn't. That was how I learned that I had a severe hearing loss. I was 25 years old. It is believed my hearing loss was a result of a series of childhood fevers and a case of mononucleosis in my early 20s. For years I was able to hear well enough with hearing aids but over the years my hearing continued to decline, and at the age of 50 it was suggested that I undergo surgery for a cochlear implant.

I was initially very resistant to this idea because I am a musician and have played the guitar (classical and fingerstyle) for over 35 years. I heard that CIs were not really good with music as they are more of a speech processor. One of my audiologists told me that I might not like the sound of music with a CI. Yet over time it was clear I was having a difficult time communicating with others. Then I went to visit a good friend who got a CI a couple of years before. As soon as I saw him, I was immediately struck by how his family was no longer speaking in sign language to him. I have known him for over 20 years and everyone always spoke in sign to him. Finally, I asked "why is no one speaking in sign language anymore?" the answer was, "because David can hear."

In January 2009 I had surgery to implant a Nucleus Freedom cochlear implant. As I have a "ski slope" type of hearing loss, there was a lot of noise in the beginning of my first months after activation. Music sounded very strange! I kept playing my guitar but the sound was not at all integrated. That is, when I struck one note on the guitar, a series of sounds resulted but it did not sound like music as I once knew it. However, music has always been the most important aspect of my life, so I was determined to not give up.

Some weeks after my activation, I began working with a music teacher friend doing some ear training exercises. We worked with tuning forks to aid me in feeling the vibrations of the pitches and frequencies of notes. In one exercise she quizzed me on interval recognition (an interval is a combination of two notes, or the distance between their pitches). She would play two notes in succession and I would listen and see if I could discern what interval it was. There are lots of song charts one can use to help with interval recognition. Examples of this are: first two notes of "Twinkle, Twinkle Little Star" is a perfect fifth, the intro to "When the Saints Go Marching In" is a major third, "Somewhere Over the Rainbow" begins with an octave, and so on. The reason this is a significant exercise is because intervals are what make up a melody. So if you are able to discern pitches by isolating them as we did in the above described exercise that can improve your ability to discern notes in a melody.

Other things we did were from a book called, *Sight Singing: Pitch, Interval, Rhythm,* by Samuel Adler. In these exercises, we worked with the piano and guitar, sounding the notes of the intervals and then singing them a cappella. The goal of these exercises were similar to the exercises in the preceding paragraph: to be able to discern intervals and to also produce them by singing. In more advanced drills, we would start by singing a series of notes in a melody out loud and then read the notes in our head silently and at the last measure of the line, sing the notes out loud again and then check with the piano to see if we stayed on pitch or not. This exercise was a lot of fun. I believe that doing these exercises really helped me regain my musical perception. My music teacher friend said that most musicians don't even do these sorts of exercises, but because many people who play an instrument hear melodies without a problem, they don't feel the need to. I still get emails from CI users all over the country asking how it is I am able to hear a melody. I hope what I described above will be helpful to others.

Six months after my activation, I got a new digital hearing aid (Phonak Naida) for my right ear. It was then I really experienced a miracle for I could then hear every note on my guitar. Before my CI and HA I could hear up to the 7th fret but now I could hear every note, all the way to the 19th fret. The difference though was that my acoustic/nylon string guitar now sounded electric. I knew it would sound different and I was prepared to accept the difference even if I didn't like it. But I was surprised that I did like the sound. Whew, what a relief and a blessing!

Now, two years later I work as a full-time professional musician. I am employed at the University of Virginia Hospital as a Certified Music Practitioner where I play therapeutic music at the bedside of hospital patients. In addition, I work for Very Special Arts (VSA) in Charlottesville,

VA, which is an organization dedicated to promote experiences in the arts for individuals with disabilities. I am the Director of Community Outreach at Music for HOPE, a non-profit organization that provides instruments for disadvantaged kids. I play regularly at assisted living centers for the elderly as well.

**Tim Polashek**—Composition and music technology professor
*Lexington, Kentucky*

I have never taken my sense of sound for granted. Inspired by my experiences as a high school musician, I pursued a career in music, obtaining a bachelor's degree from Grinnell College and a master's in electro-acoustic music at Dartmouth College. Eventually, I earned a doctorate in composition from Columbia University. I have also needed hearing aids for my entire life.

In the first grade, my teachers began noticing my irregular behavior. At times, I would speak at a volume unnecessarily loud for the classroom and in some instances communication errors would cause disagreements between me and my classmates. Soon afterward, I was diagnosed with moderate hearing loss and given a single hearing aid. In high school I received my first pair of hearing aids. I was in stereo. It was like a whole new world.

As a music technology professor, my studies have a direct relationship to daily life. Many years after studying electro-acoustic music at Dartmouth, I began using digital hearing aids, which literally allow me to experience the technology in action. My current hearing aids feature a music setting that functions much like the mastering process for digital music. By switching this setting on, I am able to hear live music as if it were filtered through a mixing board, a technological phenomena only recently available.

In fact, as I age, hearing aid technology only gets more advanced. While most people gradually lose their hearing, I get a little better every decade. My hearing loss has afforded me a rare perspective on the science of sound, beginning at an early age. As a child, I would constantly have trouble recognizing specific speech patterns. While the literal meaning behind conversations or lectures would frequently go unrecognized by my aural senses, I paid closer attention to the rhythm and tone of the human voice. Because speech often became music in my ears, I could not help but develop an interest in the art form.

Musicians with hearing loss are drawn to music because you have to think about it a little more. This unique perception of sound, as well as my interests in science, engineering and music, has led me to think about hearing loss intellectually and artistically. In 2005 I published *Beyond Babble,* an article elaborating upon my perception of sound and introducing my Beyond Babble computer program. By following a scientific equation, the program synthesizes music and poetry similar to the nonsensical music that my sense of hearing often produces in reaction to human conversation. The program produces an artificial, or constructed, language, created for an artistic purpose. By combining traditional music, technological theory and personal experiences with sound, I believe I have created something entirely original.

**Janice Rosen**—Piano, clarinet and voice student
*Washington, D.C.*

I was born with normal hearing but with malformed middle ear bones that did not grow properly. I began losing my hearing slowly as a toddler. By age six, even though my hearing loss was mild, it was severe enough that I needed to wear hearing aids to function normally.

I began learning to sing at age three or earlier with help from my dad, who was not a professional musician, but just someone who loved music and had a good voice.

I sang in my synagogue youth choir and had a very supportive choir director/music teacher who would train all of the children how to sing properly with breathing exercises and scales. My hearing aids helped me hear but my problem was in knowing how loud I would be with in comparison to the other singers in the choir. I had to listen carefully to everyone else and watch the choir director. It helped that she would sing along mouthing the words and I would lip-read in order to make sure I was keeping proper time and keeping up with everyone. I sang alto and most of the time the altos would sing very softly, too softly. I could hear the sopranos better—maybe because they were louder.

Playing the piano was frustrating when I was younger not because of hearing but because of poor coordination. I did not take formal piano lessons when I was a child even though I wanted to very much. There were no programs or teachers in my area that would accept a child with a hearing loss, much less one with other physical disabilities. I taught myself how to read music and enjoyed playing melodies with just the right hand on my family's organ. When my family would visit friends who had grand pianos it was a delight to sit and invent melodies.

I found it easier to learn to play the clarinet and recorder, as it was not necessary to have good hand coordination (at least not as much so as a piano). I played clarinet in my high school band and also some clarinet and recorder solos in programs at my synagogue when I was a teenager.

In high school I took the *Seashore Test of Musical Ability* and did very well but both my high school band teacher and my guidance counselor were very negative. They did not want me playing in the high school marching band and said that I should not think about a career in music due to my hearing loss.

In 2001 the Association of Adult Musicians with Hearing Loss (AAMHL) was founded and that opened up a whole new world for me as an amateur musician and music lover. One of the things I discovered on the AAMHL website is the Frequency to Musical Note Conversion Chart, which indicates what frequency each note on a piano keyboard is. It was what I needed in assisting me in choosing my first digital hearing aids in 2002. I showed the chart to my hearing aid dealer/audiologist and told him I wanted to be able to hear all the frequencies on a piano as well as the full range of the human singing voice—assuming that I have the auditory nerves to allow me to do this. There are no musical instruments or music testing equipment in the hearing aid dealer's office so he tested my hearing and programmed the hearing aids based on my audiogram and the Frequency to Musical Note Conversion Chart (see Appendix I).

As I live only a short distance away from his office, I went home and tried listening to the notes on my piano and CDs of singers I enjoy in order to determine if the sound is in fact "just right." I also tested the hearing aids by listening to my favorite opera singers at the Washington Opera. This was an especially useful environmental test with the *bel canto* and the flourishing *coloratura* that I know so well. However, this is not a very scientific test and I know that even with the best hearing aids I am not hearing music the same way someone with normal hearing is.

Currently I am an avid attendee at opera and classical music concerts and attend almost weekly at the Kennedy Center for the Performing Arts in Washington, D.C. I also take formal lessons in piano, clarinet and voice, and sing in a choir once a week.

Thanks to AAMHL and the many fine people and resources I have come in contact with, I have been able to revitalize my love and pursuit of music as an avocation. When I retire from my job in a few years, I hope to pursue a degree in an appropriate area of music.

## Lisa Smith—flutist
*St. Louis, Missouri*

For years family members have complained that I could not hear but I always accused them of mumbling. My father's side of the family has a hereditary hearing loss. About three years ago I asked my doctor to check my hearing so I could let my family know that my hearing was fine. To my surprise she told me the tests showed a hearing loss. I was not happy about having to tell family that they were right all along.

I saw an audiologist and was told that I had about 30% hearing in each ear and with hearing aids would have about 50%. My primary issue is clarity, not volume. I wear hearing aids, use a Ubi-Duo machine, and have studied ASL (American Sign Language). I use the Ubi-Duo machine for staff meetings at work and use an interpreter for church and when I attend our state meetings and conferences for work.

I began studying piano at age seven and started playing the flute at age nine. I received a Bachelor's of Music degree with an emphasis in piano. I no longer play the piano but play the flute with three bands, sing in the church choir, and am starting a folk music group at church.

I cannot wear my hearing aids when listening to or performing music. I am accustomed to the way music sounds for me without the hearing aids. Since bands and choirs are generally pretty loud, I can usually hear them well enough to make it work. My problem arises when the director speaks and gives direction. I generally am right in front and am able to hear enough that with lip reading I can make out what we are doing, but if I miss it, I just ask the person next to me. An interpreter would be a great help for rehearsals but the expense is prohibitive.

I also do some solo work. The only time I need to do anything special is if there is a piano accompaniment and the piano begins the piece first. Then I stand so that I can watch their hands to get the tempo and after that, they just have to follow me.

## Ali Zimmerman—Singer
*Indianapolis, Indiana*

Singing is not actually about hearing, but about feeling. The key is in knowing where to place your head, your tongue, your mouth and how you breathe. When I lost my hearing at age 25 due to autoimmune inner ear disease, I had to put my faith in that statement. A lifelong singer, I had no idea if I would ever be able to do it again. Performing in musical theatre was what I lived for and suddenly that was taken away from me. I'm forever grateful for my musical training early in life because I was able to fall back and rely on that to be able to not only enjoy music but also perform after my hearing loss.

When I'm asked about how I can possibly enjoy music now, I often tell a story about receiving a CD in the mail from my friend Mike, a musical theatre and gospel singer. He was so proud (and rightly so) of this album he had made and I was desperate to hear it. After a few days of looking at it, I got brave enough to put it in the CD player. At first I cried because I couldn't hear it, by the end I cried because what I did hear was so beautiful and I was grateful to hear it.

It took some adjustment, but I found that if I were to lie down in front of the stereo speakers so the music was coming down from above me, I could hear it slightly better and feel the vibrations in the floor. This is when I first learned about auditory memory—because I knew Mike's voice prior to my hearing loss and I knew the songs he was performing, my brain was able to recognize what it was hearing.

I equate it to muscle memory: if you break your leg and can't walk for weeks, when you are healed your muscles will remember what to do to and with enough exercise you'll be able to walk again. I learned that if I exercised my hearing with music that I knew prior to my hearing loss, I would be able to hear it. It was simply a matter of training my brain to reinterpret the signals it was getting.

Now, after almost 10 years of hearing this way and adjusting to using a very high-powered hearing aid, I am even able to enjoy new music if I am willing to put the work in to learn it. If I listen to something over and over again, preferably following along with the lyrics or sheet music, I am able to enjoy something I hadn't heard prior to my hearing loss.

Auditory memory works for me in all sorts of situations—from recognizing a song on the radio to understanding a friend from high school on the phone. It also, combined with muscle memory, is what allows me to sing again. I remember what it's supposed to feel like and I remember what it's supposed to sound like.

A big problem with hearing loss is not just the loss of volume, but more the distortion of pitches. How can you find the correct note if what you're hearing is not the same as what is being produced? Well, it isn't easy and I won't lie—it takes more practice and patience than I ever thought I had. In collaboration with Matthew Swartz, a sound designer at the Denver Center Theatre Company, I developed a system that worked to allow me to sing a leading role in live theatre again. I used the t-coil on my hearing aid with an induction loop in combination with a personal monitoring box to deliver a clear signal directly to my ear. Matt would take the signals from the microphones and band and mix them in a way that made the most sense for my brain to interpret. It took many hours with him and many headaches to get everything adjusted correctly, but when I stepped out on that stage, I was able to perform confidently and the audience had no idea I was hearing impaired.

Since working with Matt, I have again adjusted and I am now able to perform with my hearing aid programmed to a special music setting. The time I spent using the personal monitor with a specialized mix allowed me to learn the difference between the distorted pitches I was hearing and the real pitches. At the same time, I was working with a voice teacher who was able to teach me the correct positioning and breathing and feeling needed for any singer—something I had neglected prior to my hearing loss. The biggest key to hearing and enjoying music has been patience and adjustment, while the biggest key to performing again was finding people to work with and who support me in this challenge.

# Frequency to Musical Note Converter

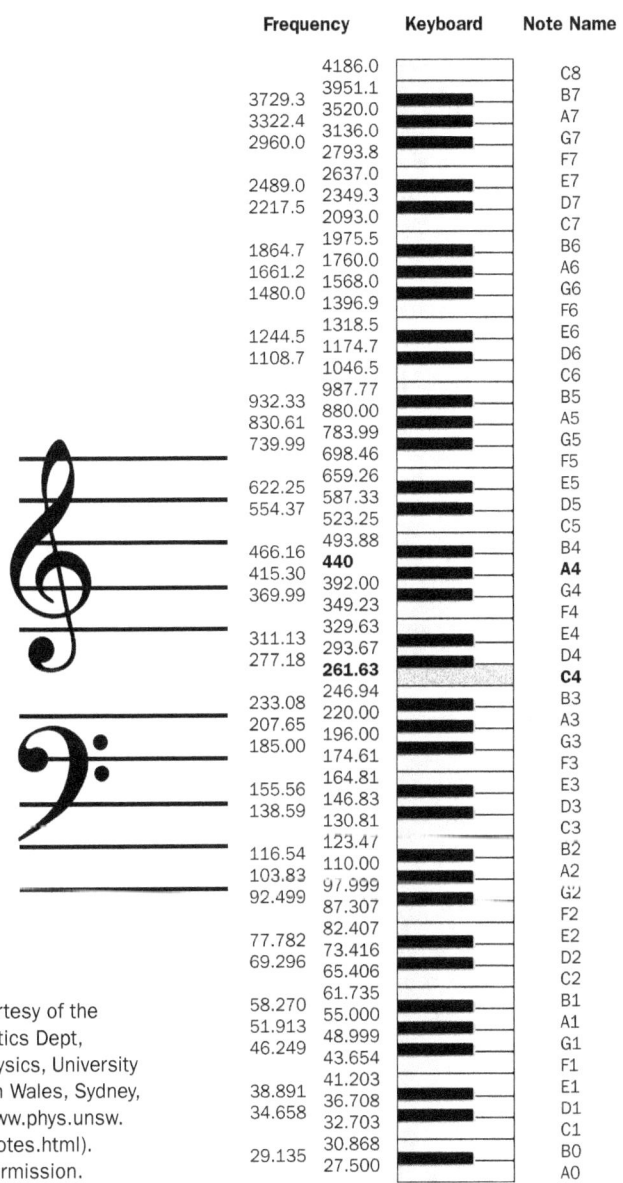

| Frequency | Keyboard | Note Name |
|---|---|---|
| 4186.0 | | C8 |
| 3729.3  3951.1 | | B7 |
| 3322.4  3520.0 | | A7 |
| 2960.0  3136.0 | | G7 |
| 2793.8 | | F7 |
| 2637.0 | | E7 |
| 2489.0  2349.3 | | D7 |
| 2217.5  2093.0 | | C7 |
| 1975.5 | | B6 |
| 1864.7  1760.0 | | A6 |
| 1661.2  1568.0 | | G6 |
| 1480.0  1396.9 | | F6 |
| 1318.5 | | E6 |
| 1244.5  1174.7 | | D6 |
| 1108.7  1046.5 | | C6 |
| 987.77 | | B5 |
| 932.33  880.00 | | A5 |
| 830.61  783.99 | | G5 |
| 739.99  698.46 | | F5 |
| 659.26 | | E5 |
| 622.25  587.33 | | D5 |
| 554.37  523.25 | | C5 |
| 493.88 | | B4 |
| 466.16  **440** | | **A4** |
| 415.30  392.00 | | G4 |
| 369.99  349.23 | | F4 |
| 329.63 | | E4 |
| 311.13  293.67 | | D4 |
| 277.18  **261.63** | | **C4** |
| 246.94 | | B3 |
| 233.08  220.00 | | A3 |
| 207.65  196.00 | | G3 |
| 185.00  174.61 | | F3 |
| 164.81 | | E3 |
| 155.56  146.83 | | D3 |
| 138.59  130.81 | | C3 |
| 123.47 | | B2 |
| 116.54  110.00 | | A2 |
| 103.83  97.999 | | G2 |
| 92.499  87.307 | | F2 |
| 82.407 | | E2 |
| 77.782  73.416 | | D2 |
| 69.296  65.406 | | C2 |
| 61.735 | | B1 |
| 58.270  55.000 | | A1 |
| 51.913  48.999 | | G1 |
| 46.249  43.654 | | F1 |
| 41.203 | | E1 |
| 38.891  36.708 | | D1 |
| 34.658  32.703 | | C1 |
| 30.868 | | B0 |
| 29.135  27.500 | | A0 |

Diagram courtesy of the
Music Acoustics Dept,
School of Physics, University
of New South Wales, Sydney,
Australia. (www.phys.unsw.
edu.au/jw/notes.html).
Used with permission.

# Resources

## Books

Behar, A., Chasin, M., and Cheesman, M., *Noise Control: A Primer.*
Singular Publishing Group: San Diego, California (September 1999).
ISBN# 1565939921

Chasin, M., *Hear the Music: Hearing Loss Prevention for Musicians.*
Self published: Toronto, Canada (2001). Currently 4th edition.
ISBN# 0920445748

_____, (Editor), *Hearing Loss in Musicians: Prevention and Management.*
Plural Publishing Inc., (2009). ISBN# 9781597561815

_____, *Musicians and the Prevention of Hearing Loss.* Singular Publishing
Group: San Diego, California, (April 1996) ISBN #156593624

_____, (Editor), *Consumer Handbook on Hearing Loss in Noise.* Auricle Ink
Publishing: Sedona, Arizona (March 2010). ISBN# 978-09825785-06

Levitin, Daniel J, *This is Your Brain On Music: The Science of a Human
Obsession.* Penguin Group Publishers: NY, NY (2007).
ISBN# 978-0452288522

## Internet Sources

### American Academy of Audiology (AAA)

http://www.asha.org
Professional organization for audiologists; contains information
for consumers on hearing loss

### Association for Adult Musicians with Hearing Loss (AAMHL)

http://www.aamhl.org
Network of amateur and professional musicians, audiologists, and music
educators with significant hearing loss. Online listserv forum for discussions
regarding how music is perceived and performed with current hearing aid and
cochlear implant technology

### Association of Late-Deafened Adults (ALDA)

http://alda.org
Organization that advocates on behalf of the 38 million Americans who have
lost some or all of their hearing

**American Speech Language Hearing Association (ASHA)**
http://www.asha.org
General information on speech language and hearing

**Better Hearing Institute**
http://www.betterhearing.org
Comprehensive information on hearing loss, tinnitus, and hearing aids

**CI Hear**
http://www.cihear.com
Internet listserv for individuals with cochlear implants

**Hearing Education and Awareness for Rockers (HEAR)**
http://www.hearnet.com
A non-profit volunteer organization dedicated to raising awareness of the real dangers of repeated exposures to excessive noise levels from music which can lead to permanent hearing loss and tinnitus

**Hearing Loss Association of America (HLAA)**
http://www.hearingloss.org
Nation's leading organization representing people with hearing loss

**Musicians Clinics of Canada (MCC)**
http://www.musiciansclinics.com

**Promenade 'Round the Cochlea**
http://www.iurc.montp.inserm.fr/cric/audition/english
Informative tutorial about the inner ear from the laboratory of Rémy Pujol in Montpellier, France

**Say What Club**
http:www.saywhatclub.com
Worldwide forum for individuals with hearing loss

# NOTES

# NOTES

# NOTES